My **Little Golden Book** About the **80s**

By Jennifer Dussling • Illustrated by Spencer Wilson

 A GOLDEN BOOK • NEW YORK

Golden Books
An imprint of Random House Children's Books
A division of Penguin Random House LLC
1745 Broadway, New York, NY 10019
penguinrandomhouse.com
rhcbooks.com

Library of Congress Control Number: 2025934103
ISBN 979-8-217-11652-2 (trade) — ISBN 979-8-217-11653-9 (ebook)
Manufactured in the United States of America
10 9 8 7 6 5 4 3 2 1
The authorized representative in the EU for product safety and compliance is Penguin
Random House Ireland, Morrison Chambers, 32 Nassau Street, Dublin D02 YH68, Ireland.
https://eu-contact.penguin.ie

reak out the boom box! Scrunch down your socks. Grab a neon jacket and tease your hair up high. It's the 1980s and anything goes!

Want to wear only one glove, covered in sparkles? Okay! A ponytail on the side of your head? Why not? You can even talk like a California Valley girl, for sure. That'd be like totally tubular, you know!

The eighties decade was so cool, so bright, people just had to wear shades. Check it out . . .

Hit toys in the 1980s seemed to pop up from anywhere. **Care Bears**, **Strawberry Shortcake**, and **Rainbow Brite** all started out as characters on greeting cards. **Teenage Mutant Ninja Turtles** began as a comic book.

Another surprise hit? With decks of question-filled cards and colorful pie-shaped playing pieces, the board game **Trivial Pursuit** was anything but trivial. It sold a record 20 million games in the United States in 1984. Everywhere, people tried to answer tough questions, like "What country did the two creators of Trivial Pursuit come from?"*

Answer: Canada

Brainy kids couldn't keep their hands off **Rubik's Cube**. Invented by Ernö Rubik, Rubik's Cube had six square sides, each broken into nine smaller squares, that could be rotated in any direction.

The goal was to keep turning and twisting until each side showed a single color. Sound easy? It's not! There are 43 *quintillion* possible combinations.

This puzzling puzzle first went on sale in the US in 1980—and it still sells well today!

The biggest toy trend of the '80s, though, was probably **Cabbage Patch Kids**. No two Cabbage Patch Kids were exactly the same. Some had freckles. Some had dimples. Some had blue eyes. Some had brown eyes. Every doll came with a unique name and adoption papers.

Xavier Roberts created the chubby-cheeked dolls, then sold the rights to Coleco, a toy company. They were a huge hit! In 1983 alone, nearly 3 million Cabbage Patch Kids were "adopted." There weren't enough to meet the demand. Reports of some badly behaved parents fighting over them in stores made the evening news.

Nothing could stop these popular dolls. In fact, in 1985, a Cabbage Patch Kid named Christopher Xavier took a trip on the US space shuttle!

Big '80s Hair

The motto for hair in the '80s was "Go big or go home"! A gravity-defying look took lots of hair spray, hair gel, and maybe a neon scrunchie or two.

The Perm

The Mullet

The Side Ponytail

The Hi-top Fade

The Mohawk

The Rattail

In 1981, America took a giant step forward when it added its first woman to the Supreme Court, **Sandra Day O'Connor**. She wasn't the only groundbreaker of the decade.

Astronaut **Sally Ride** blasted off on the space shuttle in 1983—the first American woman in space!

More women entered the workforce than ever before. They laced up their sneakers, tucked their high heels in their briefcases, and got to work!

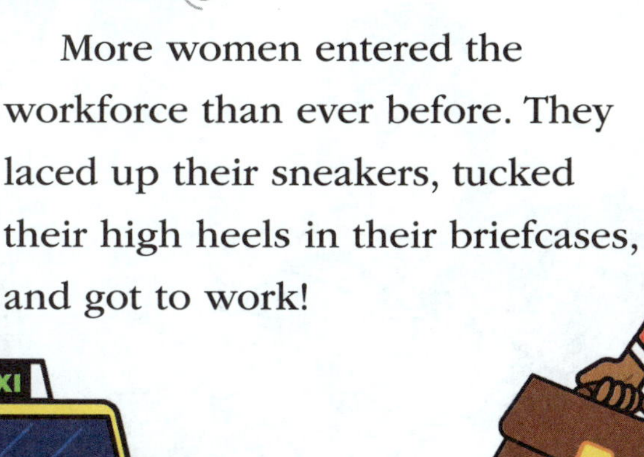

In sports, gymnast **Mary Lou Retton** stole America's heart with her huge smile and five medals at the 1984 Summer Olympics in Los Angeles. **Michael Jordan** jumped into basketball as Rookie of the Year in 1985. Quarterback **Joe Montana** helped the San Francisco 49ers dominate football, and **Wayne Gretzky** made his mark on ice hockey as the Great One.

Watching those awesome athletes inspired regular folks to shape up, too. In the 1980s, many Americans committed to getting fit. Gym memberships soared. Some women—and men—did aerobics at home to Jane Fonda's workout videos. People zipped up tracksuits and pulled on leg warmers—even when it wasn't cold. Workout clothes weren't just for working out!

While grown-ups got into fitness, kids got into video games.

On Friday nights, the coolest place to hang out was a video arcade, especially at the mall. And the coolest game to play was **Pac-Man**. Developed in Japan, *Pac-Man* started gobbling ghosts and dots in arcades across America in 1980.

Pac-Man also gobbled up space on store shelves. The hungry yellow circle was on everything, including clothes, lunch boxes, jewelry, and even shower curtains. In 1982, **Ms. Pac-Man** and her hair bow joined the Pac party.

No ride to the mall? Don't worry! Kids could play at home, too. Video game systems like Atari and Nintendo took off in the '80s, and the graphics got better and better. Some of the games are still popular today.

For entertainment on a much bigger screen, people flocked to movie theaters.

Steven Spielberg made the movies everyone wanted to watch. He had a hand in '80s faves like *Gremlins*, *Back to the Future*, and *Raiders of the Lost Ark*. But **E.T. the Extra-Terrestrial** was Spielberg's unlikely hit. This quirky blockbuster about a little alien who just wanted to go home earned over $600 million worldwide by the time it left theaters.

E.T. had the golden touch. After Reese's Pieces candies were shown in the movie, sales of the candy tripled within two weeks!

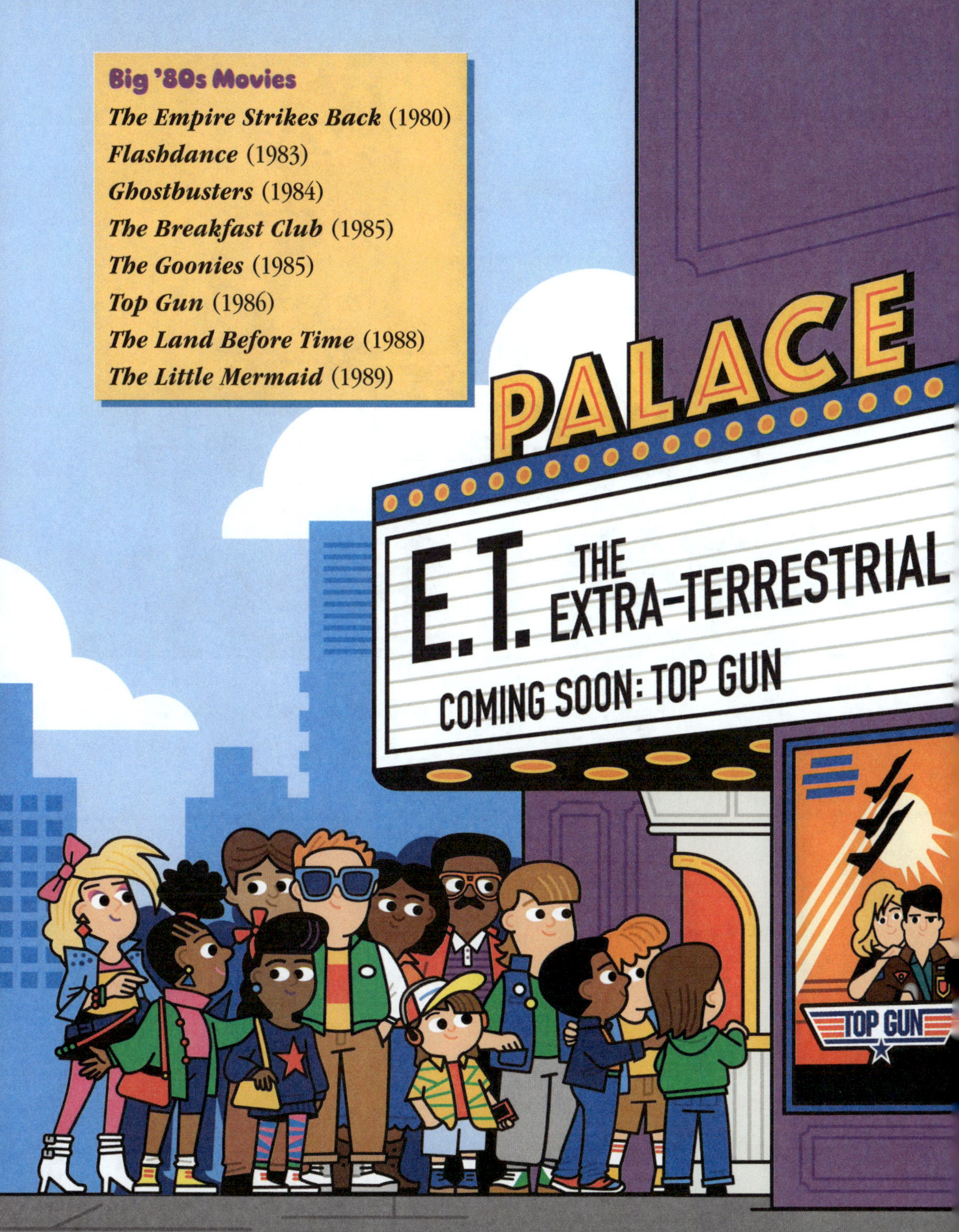

Big '80s Movies
The Empire Strikes Back (1980)
Flashdance (1983)
Ghostbusters (1984)
The Breakfast Club (1985)
The Goonies (1985)
Top Gun (1986)
The Land Before Time (1988)
The Little Mermaid (1989)
PALACE
E.T. THE EXTRA-TERRESTRIAL
COMING SOON: TOP GUN
TOP GUN

Even work got more fun in the 1980s with brand-new personal computers, or PCs for short. Computers had been around for decades, but early ones were huge. They could take up a whole room! A PC, though, was small enough to be used in homes and offices. IBM introduced one in 1981, and Apple brought out the Macintosh in 1984. Thanks to them, people could write school papers, play games, and do office work more easily. So long, typewriters!

In 1981, "princess of England" became the job every girl wanted when twenty-year-old **Diana Spencer** married **Prince Charles**, the future king of England. Their wedding was over-the-top fancy. Princess Di rode in a golden carriage pulled by horses, and the train of her dress was 25 feet long. More than 750 million people around the world turned on their TVs to watch the fairy-tale wedding.

Good thing microwave popcorn hit grocery stores that same year!

Far from England, the TV show that defined the 1980s was *Miami Vice*. Its Florida vibe, pastel colors, and Art Deco style made it cool to wear shoes without socks and blazers over T-shirts.

Plenty of other shows kept people coming back week after week. From Mr. T and kid stars to a furry alien and talking cars, '80s TV had something for everyone!

Before the 1980s, most people had three TV channels to choose from. Cable TV changed that. For the first time, viewers could choose from *dozens* of channels! CNN showed the news twenty-four hours a day. ESPN covered sports, and Nickelodeon had programs for kids. But the channel that really rocked America was MTV.

MTV—Music Television—went on the air on August 1, 1981. The channel played music videos almost nonstop, launching bands and singers into mega stardom. MTV stars didn't just make music—they also set huge fashion trends.

Madonna!
Her hit songs kept people dancing.

Bruce Springsteen!
"Born in the U.S.A." became an American anthem.

Whitney Houston!
She hit all the high notes with sweet charm and a powerful voice.

Prince!

He ruled with an album and a movie called *Purple Rain*.

Run-DMC!

Hail to the first hip-hop group to have a gold record— and a platinum one!

Boy George!

The front man for Culture Club had people wondering if he was a boy or a girl.

Music in the 1980s became 100 percent portable. People grabbed their boom boxes, popped a cassette tape into their Walkmans—and took their tunes with them. So what were '80s kids listening to?

Rebels loved fast and furious **punk** music. Most punk songs were only a couple of minutes long.

Don't let the big hair and makeup fool you—**heavy metal** groups played super-loud, hard-rocking music.

New Wave relied heavily on electric pianos, called synthesizers. The bands' looks were just as cutting edge.

Techno could sound robotic—makes sense since it was inspired by computers!

Yo! Wordplay and beats were king when it came to **rap**.

The music scene was more than dance moves and fun clothes. Big stars teamed up and wrote songs, made albums, and played shows to raise money for social causes. The absolute biggest event was **Live Aid** in 1985. This sixteen-hour-long concert was held in the United States and England at the same time and was broadcast live in 150 countries! It raised millions of dollars to fight hunger in Africa.

The '80s were bursting with bright colors, irresistible music, and originality. People could be who they wanted to be, watch what they wanted to watch, play what they wanted to play, and dance how they wanted to dance.

The 1980s were fun, fresh, and totally tubular to the max!